Come Dine With Jesus

Ten Sermons And Litanies For Lent And Easter

Robert F. Scott

CSS Publishing Company, Inc.
Lima, Ohio

BV 4277
.S39
1995

Copyright © 1995 by
CSS Publishing Company, Inc.
Lima, Ohio

Scripture quotations are from the *New Revised Standard Version of the Bible,* copyright 1989 by the Division of Christian Education of the National Council of the Churches of Christ in the USA. Used by permission.

The poem, "The Ballad of the Goodly Fere," quoted in Chapter 10, is from Ezra Pound, *Personae,* copyright 1926 by Ezra Pound. Reprinted by permission of New Directions Publishing Corporation.

Library of Congress Cataloging-in-Publication Data

Scott, Robert F., 1920-
    Come dine with Jesus : ten sermons and litanies for Lent and Easter / Robert F. Scott.
        p.   cm.
    ISBN 0-7880-0333-X
    1. Lenten sermons. 2. Holy-Week sermons. 3. Easter — Sermons. 4. Sermons, American. 5. Bible. N.T. Luke — Meditations. 6. Dinners and dining in the Bible. I. Title.
BV4277.S39   1995
252'.62—dc20   94-36281
                                                                                    CIP

This book is available in the following formats, listed by ISBN:
0-7880-0333-X Book
0-7880-0334-8 IBM 3 1/2 computer disk
0-7880-0335-6 IBM 3 1/2 book and disk package
0-7880-0336-4 Macintosh computer disk
0-7880-0337-2 Macintosh book and disk package
0-7880-0338-0 IBM 5 1/4 computer disk
0-7880-0339-9 IBM 5 1/4 book and disk package

PRINTED IN U.S.A.

To our Lord Jesus who invites us:
"I am the bread of life.
Whoever comes to me will never hunger,
and whoever believes in me will never thirst."

Table Of Contents

Preface

Why did Luke include ten occasions of Jesus sharing meals with people, seven of those scenes found only in Luke? How many hundreds or thousands of times did Jesus eat with other people? These ten occasions must have been preserved in the Christian community and related to Luke because Jesus had used them to meet deep, widespread needs or to convey important truths. Luke clearly recognized that Jesus had some purpose, some meaning to convey in these mealtime conversations.

Jesus lived and taught among people in a subsistence agrarian economy. Food occupied most of their waking hours: growing it, fishing for it, grinding it, buying and selling it, cooking it, baking it, and at last eating it. When people came together to share the joy of a wedding, food was a central part of the celebration; in a time of sorrow, gifts of food expressed condolence. It is small wonder that Jesus, with the Creator's insight to the human psyche, used food in countless illustrations. All four Gospels show this theme, and John records Jesus' discourse on himself as the bread of life. Luke gives the most specific examples; in addition to these ten meals, he includes 12 of Jesus' parables about food.

It is in these ten meals, however, that we see the importance Jesus placed on meeting people socially and interacting with them in their personal settings. In these meals we find strong bonds of affection and sharp confrontations. In the intimacy of sharing a meal, emotions come to the surface: indignation, thanksgiving, forgiveness, sorrow, overflowing joy. Jesus draws out these emotions and exposes them; he meets them with his searching insight, sometimes confirmation, sometimes deserved reproof, and always his offer of healing grace.

At the final Passover supper, Jesus took two essential parts of the Passover meal and invested them with new meaning. From then on, as long as time endures, the bread and the wine become the essential elements of the communion, the assurance of God's grace, the symbols of the new covenant. It is fitting that the ten meals in Luke be explored at communion services, for each of them expands on truths that are implicit in the communion.

These brief studies were originally written for midweek communion services during Lent. They would also be suitable for an early series on Sundays. Most could be used at communion, or in a study series without communion, at any season of the year.

I express my gratitude to the multi-denominational congregation at Ingleside Retirement Apartments, Wilmington, Delaware, who first heard these studies and encouraged me to proceed with them; to Thomas W. Lentz of CSS Publishing Company, who suggested that the litanies and visual worship focuses would make this book more useful; and to my wife Bettie, who made many helpful comments (and who should have sued my word processor for alienation of her handyman and assistant cook).

Robert F. Scott

Worship Focus

These services may be made more effective by the use of articles that illustrate Jesus' purpose at each meal. At the start of each chapter there are suggestions for these symbols.

Placement of the articles would depend on the arrangement of the room and the formality/informality of the service. The symbols could be placed on a table in the front of the room; in that case the tables should be low enough for the articles to be seen by the seated congregation. In some settings, the pastor might lift the symbols and show them to the congregation. Another possibility is to pass the articles from hand to hand through the congregation. In some buildings, a table near the entrance may be more practical.

In any setting, the symbols should be placed or handled in such a way as to focus worship on the words and actions of Jesus.

Litanies

A litany is suggested for each meal. These are coordinated with the teaching of the meals.

The First Meal

Supper With Levi
Luke 5:27-32

Worship Focus

On one side of the table, a stethoscope, for the Great Physician who came to seek the ill and the lost.

On the other side, a money bag, for the tax office Levi left behind. (Perhaps a cloth bag about a foot high, stuffed with paper to keep it upright, tied at the top with a string, a dollar sign on the front.)

A Litany For The First Meal

Leader: God of creation, we praise you, for you have brought forth life in all its beauty and complexity.

People: God of creation, we praise you for this life.

Leader: God of grace, we thank you, for you have given the breath of life to all humankind.

People: God of grace, we praise you for this life.

Leader: God of wholeness, we thank you that you have made us to be whole in body and in spirit.

People: God of wholeness, we thank you for ourselves, your gift.

Leader: God of healing, we thank you for Jesus Christ, the great physician, who came to restore our wholeness.

People: God of healing, we thank you for ourselves, your gift.

Leader: God of all grace, we thank you that in Christ you have loved us, sought us, called us to yourself, and healed our aching spirits.

People: God of creation, God of grace, God of wholeness, God of healing, we praise you for all that you are, and we thank you for all that you have made us to be. Amen.

Supper With Levi
Luke 5:27-32

Do you enjoy a meal with good friends?
  So did Jesus,
    but in the Gospels we find him sharing meals
      with a wide assortment of people:
        friends and enemies,
          pillars of society and outcasts.
Fellowship at the table was important
    in the life of our Lord.
  It led up to the climax of the Lord's Supper,
      the convincing Easter evening meals,
        the spirit-lifting breakfast at the lake.
  Luke especially stresses this;
      he records ten scenes of Jesus at meals,
        seven of them found in Luke alone.
    It's such an emphasis that one New Testament
      scholar, Robert Korris,
          even comments that the aroma of food
            penetrates the whole Gospel.

The first of these suppers is in Luke 5:27-32.
    *After this he went out and saw a tax collector
named Levi, sitting at the tax booth, and he said
to him, "Follow me." And he got up, left everything, and followed him.*
    *Then Levi gave a great banquet for him in his
house; and there was a large crowd of tax collectors and others sitting at the table with them. The
Pharisees and their scribes were complaining to his
disciples, saying, "Why do you eat and drink with
tax collectors and sinners?" Jesus answered, "Those
who are well have no need of a physician, but those
who are sick; I have come to call not the righteous
but sinners to repentance."*

What a way to start!

We think of sharing a meal together as a sign of
    friendship,
        a time for good conversation
        and pleasant experiences.
    The first meal in this Gospel is a scandal,
    and it starts a bitter, dangerous fight.

Levi was an outcast,
    a traitor, a scoundrel,
        and most probably a thief.
    He was no saint, no pillar of the church;
        in fact, the good people of the town
            wouldn't let him in the church door.
    He was one of the Jews who collected taxes
        for the hated Roman government,
        and they also collected for their own pockets —
            as much as they could.
    The rest of the Jews despised them,
        would not enter their houses,
            and most certainly would not sit down
            and eat with them.

Jesus simply said to Levi, "Follow me,"
    and Levi did.
    Then Levi, as a sign of gratitude,
        a sign of his new identity
            as Christ's new person,
        wanted to provide dinner for Jesus
            and his followers.
    But who would come?
        No good, upright, religious person
            would sit at table with Levi;
        that would make a good person un-good —
            ceremonially unclean.
    Who were left?
        Levi's friends: the other outcasts —
            tax collectors and sinners —

already considered unclean —
were the only ones
who would come to his banquet.

Only the sinners would go to Levi's feast:
    that is, only the sinners and Jesus.
    The Pharisees saw it at once:
        if this man Jesus were truly religious,
        he certainly would not eat with such riff-raff,
            associate with such scum.
        How can he claim to be a religious teacher,
            a rabbi?
        How can he pretend even to be decent?
    We all heard Jesus' answer:
        "Those who are well have no need of a physician,
            but those who are sick;
        I have come to call not the righteous
            but sinners to repentance."

Levi probably intended a joyful, friendly gathering.
    Jesus turned it into a declaration of salvation,
        the rebirth of a new Levi.
The Gospel of Jesus Christ is a Gospel of great pardons.
    It has been described as good news to the last,
        the least, and the lost.
    Right at the start, Jesus made plain
        whom he would invite to his supper:
            everyone who needed the cleansing,
                forgiving grace of God in Jesus Christ,
            everyone who wanted to be accepted by God,
                every man who was down
                    and hoped for the hand of God to lift him up,
                every woman who felt unloved
                    and longed for the love of God,
                every man or woman or child
                    who had a vision of the goodness of God
                    and who sought to live in that goodness.

Levi made a feast in his house,
    but it was the presence of Jesus
        that made it a supper of forgiveness,
          a feast of healing for the soul,
            a dinner of spiritual renewal.

In that forgiveness,
    in that healing,
        in that renewal,
          let us come now to our Lord's table.

The Second Meal

Simon: Dinner With Passion
Luke 7:36-50

Worship Focus

A cosmetic jar (perhaps one of the large plastic jars that hold shampoo or hand lotion).

A wig with long black hair (can be a cheap Halloween costume wig).

A Litany For The Second Meal

Leader: We praise you, Almighty God, for your wondrous power and glory.

People: **Praise be to you, our God Almighty!**

Leader: We praise you, God of love, for revealing yourself through Christ our Lord.

People: **Praise be to you, our God of love!**

Leader: We praise you, for in Jesus Christ you have accomplished our redemption.

People: **Praise be to God, for freeing us from sin.**

Leader: We praise you, for in Jesus Christ you have forgiven us and made us new.

People: **Praise be to God, for making us new.**

Leader: We thank you, for in Christ you have called us to yourself.

People: **Praise be to God, who calls us in love.**

Leader: You have made us your new people, the family of Christ.

People: **Praise be to God, who enfolds us in love.**

All: **Praise and thanksgiving and glory and love be to our God, who has loved us, forgiven us, renewed us, and set us free. Amen.**

Simon: Dinner With Passion
Luke 7:36-50

Jesus shared his meals with such varied people
    that often there were strong emotional overtones.
Luke brings us ten of these table scenes,
    and we find some indication
        of the importance they must have had to Jesus.

The first dinner was at the house of Levi,
    a despised tax collector,
    and at once the Pharisees severely criticized Jesus,
        saying no decent rabbi
        would associate with such an outcast.
Jesus answered them,
    "Those who are well have no need of a physician,
        but those who are sick.
    I have come not to call the righteous,
        but sinners to repentance."

The second dinner, surprisingly,
    was at the other end of the social
        and religious scale.
We find it in Luke 7:36-50
    One of the Pharisees asked Jesus to eat with him,
    and he went into the Pharisee's house and took his
    place at the table.
The Pharisees were very religious,
    trying to live by every detail of the rabbinic laws,
    and they were highly respected by the people.
We don't know whether this Pharisee
    was beginning to believe in Jesus
        or whether he just wanted to examine
        the new teacher.
Whatever his motive,
    trouble entered that room at once.

And a woman in the city, who was a sinner, having learned that he was eating in the Pharisee's house, brought an alabaster jar of ointment. She stood behind him at his feet, weeping, and began to bathe his feet with her tears and to dry them with her hair. Then she continued kissing his feet and anointing them with the ointment. Now when the Pharisee who had invited him saw it, he said to himself, "If this man were a prophet, he would have known who and what kind of woman this is who is touching him — that she is a sinner."

It was normal for a servant to wash the feet
　　of an invited guest.
It was definitely not normal for a harlot
　　to enter the house of a Pharisee,
　　　　where she would be decidedly unwelcome.
It was even more abnormal
　　for her to wash a rabbi's feet with her tears.
A strict rabbi would not speak to a woman
　　in public
　　not even the most upright woman.
Surely, if this man were a prophet,
　　he would not let this sinner touch him.
But Jesus met the Pharisee's objection:
　　he not only knew the woman's character;
　　　　he read the Pharisee's innermost thoughts.

Jesus spoke up and said to him, "Simon, I have something to say to you." "Teacher," he replied, "Speak." "A certain creditor had two debtors; one owed five hundred denarii, and the other fifty. When they could not pay, he canceled the debts for both of them. Now which of them will love him more?" Simon answered, "I suppose the one for whom he canceled the greater debt." And Jesus said to him, "You have judged rightly." Then turning

*toward the woman, he said to Simon, "Do you see
this woman? I entered your house; you gave me no
water for my feet, but she has bathed my feet with
her tears and dried them with her hair. You gave
me no kiss, but from the time I came in she has not
stopped kissing my feet. You did not anoint my head
with oil, but she has anointed my feet with
ointment."*

Note that in Jesus' parable,
    love is the result of forgiveness.
  Then Jesus took this principle,
     to which the Pharisee had agreed,
    and applied it to the situation at that table.
"Simon," he said,
   "You didn't even give me
     the ordinary everyday courtesies,
    but this woman,
     whom you despise,
      has done so much more than ordinary.
   Why?
    Because she has found forgiveness,
    and her inward assurance
     of the forgiveness of sin
   is now being expressed
     in these outward actions of love."

*"Therefore, I tell you, her sins, which were many,
have been forgiven; hence she has shown great love.
But the one to whom little is forgiven, loves little."
Then he said to her, "Your sins are forgiven." But
those who were at table with him began to say among
themselves, "Who is this who even forgives sins?"
And he said to the woman, "Your faith has saved
you; go in peace."*

21

Everyone knew it was a staggering claim.
    Only God can forgive sins.
Jesus unabashedly asserted his status
      as God incarnate.
    Notice what he said.
      She was saved through faith,
        not through love.
      Many scholars think the woman
        may have already met Jesus,
          believed in him,
          and asked his forgiveness.
    In his grace and compassion,
      he offered forgiveness;
        by faith she accepted his gift.
    Now she was a new person,
      able to demonstrate her response of love.
    She could go in peace:
      peace with God,
        peace in her own heart.

The story is charged with emotion.
    Jesus' correction of Simon,
      his tender reception of the sinner,
        the eloquence of her silent actions,
          all fit into the picture of God's concern.
The living God is not indifferent;
    God loved the world so passionately
      that God sent the only son —
      sent him so that everyone who believes in him
        should not perish but should have eternal life.
    This God is passionately interested in people:
      people in need,
      people in pain,
      people in sorrow,
      people and their hopes,
        their loves,
          their ambitions,

people in their experiences of sin,
anxiety,
and lostness.
In this love Jesus came to seek the lost,
forgive the sinner,
wipe away the anxieties.

This is the good news of the Gospel:
that God has given this love freely.
God has not doled love out grudgingly
to the righteous,
drop by drop as they have slowly earned it;
God has poured it out abundantly
to those who come to the Savior in faith,
confessing their sin,
asking his forgiveness,
responding to his love.

The good news of Jesus was the same
for the outcast and for the social leader
for the open sinner
and for those who seemed upright;
God's passionate love and rich forgiveness —
Jesus' love for Levi,
and Levi's response of love by making a feast —
Jesus' love for Simon the Pharisee —
and will Simon return that love?

This much was plain
at the house of Simon the Pharisee,
and true in this room today:
when the Lord is at his table,
it is a focus of passion and compassion,
a place for God's forgiveness
and our human response of love.

The Third Meal

5,000 For Supper?
Luke 9:10-17

Worship Focus

Tray with five small loaves, about the size of crusty dinner rolls, and two small fish. (Ethnic groceries and some supermarkets have dried fish or whole small smoked fish. One might also use plastic fish intended for a child's bathtub.)

223976

A Litany For The Third Meal

(Based on Psalm 104 and John 6)

Leader: We give thanks to you, God of all creation, who brings forth food from the earth.

People: Grass for the cattle and grain for the mill,

Leader: Wine to gladden the human heart, oil to make the face shine,

People: And bread to strengthen the human heart.

Leader: We give thanks to you for Jesus our Redeemer, the living bread come down from heaven.

People: Lord, give us this bread always.

Leader: We thank you for your promise: the one who comes to Jesus shall not hunger, and the one who believes in him shall never thirst.

People: Lord, feed us always on the bread of life.

Leader: In your great abundance you have provided for our bodies.

People: We pray for those who have not shared in this abundance.

Leader: In great mercy you have provided the living bread for our souls.

People: We pray for those who are hungry for that heavenly bread.

All: Keep us ever mindful of your abundance and your compassion; guide us so to use your gifts that we shall be agents of your compassion. Amen.

5,000 For Supper
Luke 9:10-17

Did a member of your family ever come home,
>   just at supper time, and casually announce,
"By the way,
>   I've brought home a few friends for supper,
>   only about twelve" —
>   but you didn't have anything prepared?
When Jesus dumped this surprise on his disciples,
>   it wasn't a dozen extra people:
>   it was 5,000!

We read in the Gospel according to Luke
>   that Jesus had sent the twelve apostles
>   out into the villages to preach and to heal.
When they returned,
>   ready to tell of all they had seen and done,
Jesus took them off into the wilderness,
>   possibly to rest;
>   but they had spread Jesus' fame,
>   and the crowds were determined to see him.

> ... *he welcomed them, and spoke to them about
> the kingdom of God, and healed those who needed
> to be cured.*
> *The day was drawing to a close, and the twelve
> came to him and said, "Send the crowd away, so
> that they may go into the surrounding villages and
> countryside, to lodge and get provisions; for we are
> here in a deserted place." But he said to them, "You
> give them something to eat." They said, "We have
> no more than five loaves and two fish — unless we
> are to go and buy food for all these people." For
> there were about five thousand men. And he said
> to his disciples, "Make them sit down in groups of*

about fifty each." They did so and made them all sit down. And taking the five loaves and the two fish, he looked up to heaven, and blessed and broke them, and gave them to the disciples to set before the crowd. And all ate and were filled. What was left over was gathered up, twelve baskets of broken pieces.

It was the end of a long day.
    People were tired and hungry,
        and the disciples suggested that Jesus
        send the crowd away to buy food.
The disciples were concerned about the people,
    but they realized their own helplessness
        in the face of such a great need.
    To their surprise,
        Jesus said,
            "You do it.
            You are concerned about the people,
                rightly so.
            Now act on your concern.
            You feed them."
Jesus knew that they could not do it,
    and he knew already what he would do.
    He knew, also, that there is a lesson
        we human beings must learn:
        that we are not God,
        that before God can act through us,
            we must acknowledge our own helplessness.
The disciples said simply,
    "There's nothing we can do.
All we have is five barley loaves
        and two little fish —
    that's nothing for a crowd this big."
(It is in John's Gospel that we learn
    a boy had given the loaves and the fish,
    all that he had.)

Once the disciples had admitted
        they were powerless,
            Jesus trusted them with the work.
    He did not hog the spotlight;
        he gave the disciples a role,
            seating the people in groups
            and distributing the bread and fish.
    We don't know the details.
    All we know is that this is the only miracle
        reported in all four Gospels:
        that after Jesus had looked up to heaven
                and offered the blessing,
            there was enough for everyone to eat
            and be satisfied.
        Then, in respect for God's gift of bread —
            and to show the abundance of the gift —
            they took up 12 baskets of food
            that remained.

This is the third of the meals
    recorded in the Gospel of Luke.
    At Levi's feast,
        Jesus was the guest of honor;
    at the Pharisee's dinner,
        Jesus was a guest but was not honored.
    Now, out in the wilderness,
        Jesus takes his place as host.
    From beginning to end,
        Jesus is the center of the event.
    He creates the situation,
        he arranges the meal,
        he breaks the bread and divides the fish,
        and through his hands the miracle unfolds.

The crowd came there as sheep without a shepherd.
Jesus presented himself as the shepherd
    who provides for their needs.

There, in the simplicity of bread and fish,
the true shepherd revealed himself to his sheep.

The Christian life is always a pilgrimage,
always a path through the wilderness,
always a life of dependence
on the one who can do all things,
even when we are most helpless.
Yet, as we come to the Lord's table,
let us also remember
that our Lord uses the gifts of his people,
that nothing happened then
until a young lad gave his supper,
and that nothing happens in our lives now
until we give ourselves to Christ.
The disciples knew that the task was too great
for their own strength,
but it was through their hands —
and ours —
that God acts,
to spread God's blessings and gifts
to all who will receive them.

The Fourth Meal

Martha's Supper; Mary's Feast
Luke 10:38-42

Worship Focus

On one side of the table, a jumble of cooking pots, some on top of others at crazy angles.

On the other side, an open Bible.

A Litany For The Fourth Meal

Leader: God of all wisdom, we thank you that you call us to yourself.

People: **God of all mercy, we thank you that you invite us to bring to you our prayers.**

Leader: God of all knowledge, our lives are always open before you.

People: **God of compassion, open our eyes, that we may see our inward needs.**

Leader: We come as people who want to know you and serve you.

People: **We come as those who do not always clearly hear your voice.**

Leader: Often we are bogged down in daily cares, too busy to listen for your word.

People: **We blame others for our problems and pains, and we forget to forgive one another.**

Leader: Other times we fail in our responsibilities to each other;

People: **We become the source of strife, when we should be bearers of your love.**

Leader: Free us from ourselves, so that we may feel your loving care and may walk in your pathways.

People: **Teach us to face each new day with your life and hope in our hearts.**

Leader: Thus may we find your will for our lives.

People: **This we pray through Jesus Christ, our Redeemer and our Lord. Amen.**

Martha's Supper; Mary's Feast
Luke 10:38-42

When Jesus was present at a supper,
  often he brought out the problems
    of the people there,
  and he had a way of meeting their needs
    and healing their relationships.

In the House of Simon the Pharisee,
  when a woman of the streets
    washed Jesus' feet with her tears,
  the encounter brought out
    the woman's sinfulness;
  it also exposed Simon's self-righteousness
    and the smallness of his love.
There was healing for the woman,
  for Jesus said her sins were forgiven;
and there was healing also for Simon,
  as Jesus pointed him
    to a richer meaning of love.

In the fourth supper, there was again
  both conflict and healing.
we find this in Luke, Chapter 10.

> *Now as they went on their way, he entered a certain village, where a woman named Martha welcomed him into her home. She had a sister named Mary, who sat at the Lord's feet and listened to what he was saying. But Martha was distracted by her many tasks; so she came to him and asked, "Lord, do you not care that my sister has left me to do all the work by myself? Tell her then to help me." But the Lord answered her, "Martha, Martha, you are worried and distracted by many things; there is*

need of only one thing. Mary has chosen the better
part, which will not be taken away from her."

When Jesus went to supper at Martha's house,
   the tension between Martha and her sister
      came out into the open.
Martha finally burst out,
     "Lord, do you not care that my sister
       has left me to do all the work by myself?
   Tell her to help me."

Had Jesus caused the dissension?
   No, I believe he exposed the tension
     that was already there,
       festering in the family relationship
         between two very different personalities.
   Year after year
     the sisters had grown up together,
       with different ways of looking at things,
       different sets of values,
       until finally this supper was just too much,
       and Martha blew up.

Each of the sisters was, as we all are,
       a mixture of sensitivity and insensitivity.
   We see Mary's insensitivity to Martha's need
     for help to feed their guests,
     Martha's insensitivity to Mary's need
      to feed the soul.
Martha was sensitive to hospitality:
     in the custom of the day,
       she tried to do all she could
       to make a feast worthy of such a guest;
   but she failed to realize
     that Jesus preferred a chance to teach.
Mary was sensitive to the word of God.
   She perceived that Jesus

found his plain spiritual truth
more important than a fancy meal,
but she failed to realize her duty as hostess
and her responsibility
not to leave the whole burden
on her sister Martha.

Martha's outburst finally exposed the differences,
and it opened the sisters
to Jesus' words of healing.
Gently he rebuked Martha,
pointing out that he was more interested
in helping people than in having a big banquet.
Yet, in mentioning Martha's burdens,
he indirectly chided Mary
for not helping her sister.
Then he effectively invited them both to sit,
to listen,
to forget the busy-ness,
to open themselves to the word of God,
to share together in God's peace.

There was healing.
There must have been healing,
for we meet the sisters later, together.
At the death of their brother Lazarus,
Martha was the first to run out to meet Jesus.
Mary, quieter, came a few minutes later;
both spoke to the Lord out of the same faith.
Still later, at supper in Lazarus' house,
Martha, always the more active,
served the supper;
Mary anointed Jesus' feet.
Each retained her own personality:
Martha active, doing things,
Mary more contemplative, quieter,
but they were together.

The one-time rift between them had been healed —
  healed by the Jesus who invites us all,
    now,
    to renew our spirits with his healing grace.

The Fifth Meal

Supper Etiquette
Luke 11:37-42

Worship Focus

A pitcher and a wash basin. A matched set, so common in nineteenth century bedrooms, would be ideal. If that is unavailable, use any large ceramic pitcher and wide flat bowl.

A Litany For The Fifth Meal

Leader: Glorious are you, O God, in your holiness.

People: Holy, holy, holy is our Almighty God.

Leader: Spotless and without blemish, O Christ, are you in your purity.

People: Holy, holy, holy is the Christ, our Redeemer.

Leader: Blameless and without flaw are you, Holy Spirit.

People: Holy, holy, holy is the Holy Spirit who sustains us.

Leader: We thank you, Holy God, that you have reached down to us in our imperfections.

People: Wash us, and we shall be clean.

Leader: We praise you, Gracious God, for forgiveness so freely offered in Jesus Christ.

People: Cleanse us, that we may be your renewed people.

All: Glorious and holy is our God, God of heaven and of earth, who has washed us and made us clean. Keep us, O God, in your way of holiness. Amen.

Supper Etiquette
Luke 11:37-42

When you are invited to dinner,
    you probably do not try to embarrass your host
    or to scold him.
Yet Jesus did just that,
    and I believe he did it
      in an effort to help the host.

While he was speaking, a Pharisee invited him to dine with him; so he went in and took his place at the table. The Pharisee was amazed to see that he did not first wash before dinner.

Why should the Pharisee be so astonished?
    Weren't Jesus' hands clean?
Remember that this was not just washing
    our hands as you and I might do.
The Pharisees had elevated hand-washing
    to an elaborate ritual.
Water was kept in special stoneware jars.
The amount of water used must be
    at least enough to fill one and a half eggshells.
First the water must be poured over the hands,
    beginning at the fingertips
      and running to the wrist.
Then each hand must be cleansed
    by rubbing with the other fist.
Finally,
    water must be poured over the hands again,
    this time beginning at the wrist
      and running down to the fingertips.
One must not omit even the slightest detail.

Jesus ignored the ritual,
   and the Pharisee was amazed.
He expected a religious man,
   a teacher,
      to observe the proper customs.
Was this a careless breach of etiquette?
   I believe Jesus broke the rule deliberately
      to show the emptiness of such ceremonies
         and to create an opportunity for teaching.

The Pharisee had wanted to get a better look
   at this Jesus.
He didn't realize that Jesus
   would have a better look at him:
that, in fact,
   Jesus would look right through him.
When the Pharisee raised his eyebrows,
   Jesus answered with a strong admonition

*Then the Lord said to him, "Now you Pharisees
clean the outside of the cup and of the dish, but in-
side you are full of greed and wickedness. You fools!
Did not the one who made the outside make the in-
side also? So give for alms those things that are within; and see, everything will be clean for you.*

*"But woe to you Pharisees! For you tithe mint and
rue and herbs of all kinds, and neglect justice and
the love of God; it is these you ought to have prac-
ticed, without neglecting the others."*

Was it rude of Jesus to scold his host?
   He had to do his father's business;
      it would be unfaithful of him
         not to correct the Pharisee.

When Jesus was invited to dinner,
   he had a way of exposing needs
      and bringing healing.

He showed the absurdity of attaching
   such importance to the cleansing of the body,
      while the cleansing of the spirit was overlooked.
   "Give the things that are within you," he taught,
   "the offering of the inward person.
      Give your heart,
         your affections,
         and your will to God,
         as the first great gift;
            that is the primary need.
      When you have done that,
         then all your other actions,
         proceeding from a right spirit,
            will be an acceptable worship for God."
   The prophets had said this before.
   Jesus,
      who alone is able to judge our hidden thoughts,
         was able to apply it directly
            to the person who needed it.

Jesus exposed the need;
      and did it lead to healing?
Jesus opened the way.
   When he said, "Woe to you Pharisees,"
      he used a word for "woe"
         that can mean sorrow or yearning.
      In effect, Jesus said, "I grieve for you ..."
      Jesus called on his host to realize
         what is important.
We can hope for this Pharisee,
      for wise persons welcome correction
         when it is in order.
   The Gospels tell us that many of the Pharisees
      became believers in Christ.
Certainly we know that there has been healing
   in this incident for many generations of souls,
      who have learned that if first
         the inner person is cleansed,

then outward love will flow
    in worship that is rich and true.

What does it mean for you and me
    to sit at Christ's table?
When you and I invite guests to dinner,
    we want the house clean,
        the table attractive,
        the food well prepared,
        the decorations tasteful.
But to make our guests comfortable,
    it is even more important
        that we welcome them
            with sincere friendship,
            with concern for their well-being,
            with a desire to please them
                and to do what they would like.
Our genuine love and concern
    for our guests' feelings
are more important
    than the externals of the room.
When we are at table with Jesus,
    it is even more important,
        not that the externals are right or wrong,
        but that they come from inner feelings
            that are right.
What matters is our love for Christ,
    our inward desire for his forgiveness,
    our intention to strive for his holiness,
        an inner holiness that comes
            only by the grace of God.
We want to worship him with dignity
    and with beauty.
    This is right; it is very right.
    But let us first offer him our love
        and seek his righteousness;
    then the beauty and the dignity
        will truly be an offering of worship to God.

The Sixth Meal

A Strange Invitation
Luke 14:1-6

Worship Focus

A toy animal and a doll. One of the fake sheep made for yard decorations would be ideal; the doll should be of comparable size.

Or a challah, the large braided loaf of white bread that is often part of a Jewish Sabbath meal.

A Litany For The Sixth Meal

Leader: O God, we thank you for your matchless love, by which you sent Christ to be our savior.

People: **In love you call us to yourself and hold us in your hands.**

Leader: We confess that too often our hearts are cold and without gratitude.

People: **Too often our hands are passive, and we fail to do your acts of mercy.**

Leader: Too often our lips are sealed tightly, unwilling to speak words of love.

People: **Too often we are separated from you and alienated from others.**

Leader: Yet you have promised never to forsake us.

People: **Assure us, we pray, that you have not abandoned us.**

Leader: You are the great physician; heal us now, we pray.

People: **May your table be to us a place of hope.**

Leader: Warm us with your grace,

People: **And make us agents of your love, through Jesus Christ our Lord. Amen.**

A Strange Invitation
Luke 14:1-6

Jesus received a strange invitation.
The main Sabbath meal took place about noon,
    after worship,
      and it was a normal custom
        to invite visiting teachers to dine.
Yet one Sabbath Jesus received an invitation
    that was far from normal.
    Why was Jesus invited,
      and why did he go?

> *On one occasion, when Jesus was going to the house
> of a leader of the Pharisees to eat a meal on the Sab-
> bath, they were watching him closely. Just then, in
> front of him, there was a man who had dropsy.*

Why did the Pharisee invite Jesus?
It was a trap.
Jesus had already upset the Pharisees
    by breaking their Sabbath regulations.
    Luke had previously told
      of three marvelous healings on the Sabbath,
        including two right in the synagogue
        in front of the Pharisees:
          a man with a withered hand
          and a woman with a crippled back.
    Healing was considered work,
      and all work was unlawful on the Sabbath.
    The Pharisees were shocked and angry
      that Jesus had defiled the holy day
        by such Sabbath-breaking.

When Jesus came to dinner,
    the Pharisees were watching.

The word for "watching" is the same word
that is used for espionage.
Jesus was under surveillance.
A sick man, all swollen with dropsy or edema,
had been planted there
to see what Jesus would do.
If Jesus broke the Sabbath again,
there would be official witnesses.

We know why the invitation was given,
but why did Jesus go?
This is the third time Luke shows Jesus
at dinner with a Pharisee.
The first time, Jesus was criticized
because a harlot came in
and washed his feet with her tears.
He responded by declaring her sins forgiven.
The second time, Jesus was criticized
for not washing his hands in the ritual way.
He replied that the true gift to God
is a life cleansed from within.

This third time, Jesus knew at once it was a trap.
Why would he go?
He went because he would not abandon any person.
By going,
he could offer the sick man healing for his body;
by going,
he could offer the Pharisees healing
for their souls.
People might be hostile,
they might be indifferent;
Jesus still went to them,
appealed to them,
longed for them,
hoped for them,
gave them a chance to respond to God.

And Jesus asked the lawyers and Pharisees, "Is it lawful to cure people on the sabbath, or not?" But they were silent. So Jesus took him and healed him, and sent him away.

Everyone knew the answer.
  The law allowed emergency care on the Sabbath
      if there was immediate danger of death,
    but a long-term illness must wait
      for a workday.
  The Pharisees weren't there to find answers;
    they were there to find an accusation.

Jesus gave them what they were looking for.
  Then he said to them, "If one of you has a child or an ox that has fallen into a well, will you not immediately pull it out on a sabbath day?" And they could not reply to this.

He challenged them with their own rules.
  Palestine had many open wells and pits;
      it was not uncommon for an animal to fall in,
    and the rules permitted a man
        to care for a poor animal in such a case.
  Jesus' words were unanswerable.
  If it is right to help an animal on the Sabbath day,
      how can it be wrong to help a man?
    What is worth more:
      a person or an ox?

At the Pharisee's table,
  Jesus declared the importance of people:
    both the sick man and the Pharisee.
  He did not give up on the Pharisees;
    only they themselves could remove them
      from the grace of God.

And likewise, God does not give up on us;
only we can resist God's love.
Whatever and wherever we are,
God's mercy and God's concern
will reach out to us.

The table of Jesus Christ
is a table of healing and of hope.
It was a place of healing for the man
swollen with dropsy;
it was a place of hope — God's hope —
for the Pharisee.

The table of Jesus Christ is still,
for you and for me,
a place of healing and a place of hope.
Let us so come
that we may find healing for our souls
and hope for each new day.

The Seventh Meal

Thanksgiving In Jericho
Luke 19:1-10

Worship Focus

A large bowl or basket of fruit; a pedestal bowl would be festive.

Jericho was known as the City of Palms, so an arrangement of dates would also be in order.

A Litany For The Seventh Meal

Leader: God of all power, we praise you, for you tower above all other loyalties.

People: **Now is the acceptable time.**

Leader: God of all grace, we thank you for the gift of salvation through Jesus Christ.

People: **Now is the day of salvation!**

Leader: God of all majesty, we thank you once more that you have called us to yourself.

People: **Now is the acceptable time.**

Leader: God of all mercy, we adore you, for you have loved us and forgiven us.

People: **Now is the day of salvation.**

Leader: God of all life, we live because you live and have given us new life in Christ.

People: **Now has salvation come to this house. Now is the day of new life. Let the people of God give praise! Amen.**

Thanksgiving In Jericho
Luke 19:1-10

*He entered Jericho and was passing through it. A
man was there named Zacchaeus; he was a chief tax
collector and was rich. He was trying to see who
Jesus was, but on account of the crowd he could
not, because he was short in stature. So he ran ahead
and climbed a sycamore tree to see him, because he
was going to pass that way. When Jesus came to the
place, he looked up and said to him, "Zacchaeus,
hurry and come down; for I must stay at your house
today." So he hurried down and was happy to wel-
come him. All who saw it began to grumble and said,
"He has gone to be the guest of one who is a sinner." Zacchaeus stood there and said to the Lord,
"Look, half of my possessions, Lord, I will give to
the poor; and if I have defrauded anyone of anything, I will pay back four times as much." Then
Jesus said to him, "Today salvation has come to this
house, because he too is a son of Abraham. For the
Son of Man came to seek out and to save the lost."*

Jesus entered Jerusalem on what we call
   Palm Sunday with a great, festive procession.
Before him and behind him surged crowds
   of pilgrims on their way to the Passover,
     shouting praises,
     waving palm branches,
     throwing their garments
       for him to ride upon,
     hailing him as a deliverer,
     shouting "Hosanna to the Son of David."
       "Blessed is the King who comes
         in the name of the Lord."
   The whole city was stirred, asking,
     "Who is this?"

51

Yet Palm Sunday was not Jesus' first
    great procession on the trip to Jerusalem,
    nor were these the first palms.
A week earlier Jesus had been in Jericho,
    often called "The City of Palms."
Jericho was wealthy,
    both from its date palms
    and even more from the main trade routes
    that ran through the city.
One of Jericho's wealthiest men
    lived by taxing that trade:
    he was also its most hated man,
    the chief tax collector Zacchaeus.

Jesus' entrance to Jericho
    was truly a festive parade.
The excited, cheering crowd filled the streets
    so you could hardly find Jesus.
We all know the story of little Zacchaeus
    who climbed a tree.
He was lonely;
    he knew he was detested and despised.
He had heard of that strange Rabbi Jesus:
    most rabbis would never speak to a person
    like Zacchaeus,
    but this Jesus
    was said to be a friend of sinners.
Zacchaeus was desperate,
    but the crowd was in the way,
        probably happy to push him aside
        and give him an extra shove.
Abandoning all dignity, he climbed a tree —
    and you know the rest.
Jesus invited himself to Zacchaeus' house
    for dinner.

The grumbling started at once.
  Zacchaeus was a sinner,
    hated because he collected taxes
      for the Roman government
    and hated even more
      because he collected extra for himself.
  How dare a rabbi associate with such a sinner,
    even eat with him
      and his fellow scoundrels?
  What was going on?

You know what was going on!
  It was Thanksgiving Day!
  That dinner in Zacchaeus' house
    was a great big thanksgiving feast:
      no turkey,
        no cranberries,
          but great thanksgiving!
  It was the thanksgiving of an outcast,
    long friendless,
      now accepted by the love of God.

Thanksgiving, to mean anything,
    has to be more than words.
  Thanksgiving in Zacchaeus' house
    was a time for action.
  He began with repentance;
    next came restitution,
    a generous restitution.
      (The law required a thief, if caught,
        to pay back double;
      Zacchaeus, repentant,
        paid back fourfold.)
  Then there could be renewal.
  Zacchaeus' whole life-style changed
    from me-first money-grubbing
      to an outgoing care for others,

53

"Half of my possessions, Lord,
I will give to the poor."

Palm procession in Jericho,
Palm Sunday in Jerusalem:
both were times of renewal.
The encounter in Jericho
brought restoration to Zacchaeus;
the celebration in Jerusalem
was a step in Jesus' plan
of redemption for us all.
When Jesus sat at table
with the sinners of Jericho,
salvation blossomed into actions
of thanksgiving.
Then the Savior entered Jerusalem
with cheers and the waving of palms,
in order to spread for us a continuing table
of forgiveness and rebirth,
of thanksgiving and service,
of rejoicing and praise.

The Eighth Meal

Supper Of Desire
Luke 22:7-20

Worship Focus

A plate of matzoth (for this was the Passover, the feast of unleavened bread) and a chalice.

A Litany For The Eighth Meal

Leader: Gracious God, we gather in remembrance of the Passover Jesus shared with his disciples.

People: **We remember that night.**

Leader: We remember that Jesus washed the feet of his disciples as a sign of his love for them.

People: **We remember the many signs of his love for us.**

Leader: We thank you for the broken bread, the symbol of Jesus' body, broken for us.

People: **We remember him in the broken bread.**

Leader: We thank you for the cup, the symbol of Jesus' sacrifice for us.

People: **We remember him in the cup.**

Leader: We are humbled, loving God, as we remember Jesus' prayer in the garden, his arrest, his trial, and his suffering.

People: **We remember that his suffering was for our redemption.**

All: **We remember this night, and we praise you, O God, for the life of Jesus and his presence with us now. Amen.**

Supper Of Desire
Luke 22:7-20

Then came the day of unleavened bread, on which the Passover lamb had to be sacrificed. So Jesus sent Peter and John, saying, "Go and prepare the Passover meal for us so that we may eat it." They asked him, "Where do you want us to make preparations for it?" "Listen," he said to them, "When you have entered the city, a man carrying a jar of water will meet you; follow him into the house he enters and say to the owner of the house, 'The teacher asks you, "Where is the guest room where I may eat the Passover with my disciples?" ' He will show you a large room upstairs, already furnished. Make preparations for us there." So they went and found everything as he had told them; and they prepared the Passover meal.

When the hour came, he took his place at the table, and the apostles with him. He said to them, "I have eagerly desired to eat this Passover with you before I suffer; for I tell you, I will not eat it again until it is fulfilled in the kingdom of God." Then he took a cup, and after giving thanks he said, "Take this and divide it among yourselves; for I tell you that from now on I will not drink the fruit of the vine until the kingdom of God comes." Then he took a loaf of bread, and when he had given thanks, he broke it and gave it to them, saying, "This is my body, which is given for you. Do this in remembrance of me." And he did the same with the cup after supper, saying, "This cup that is poured out for you is the new covenant in my blood."

Jesus' words express unusual emphasis,
    doubling the word for desire;
  they might be translated,
    "With desire have I desired
      to eat this passover with you."
This is the central supper,
    found in all four Gospels;
  it is a supper for which Jesus
    had a definite purpose.

The Gospel of Luke shows Jesus at supper
  with all sorts of people:
    outcasts like Levi and Zacchaeus,
    honored Pharisees and learned scribes,
    women of the streets,
    neighbors who crowd in to listen,
    the highest and lowest of society,
    those who come to adore him
      and those who set a trap to entangle him.

Now we come to a different supper.
  This is the supper Jesus desired,
    and it gives meaning to all of the others.
Jesus makes the transition from guest to host.
  He is not with strangers who invited him
    or who dropped in from the streets.
  He has planned the place and the time;
    he has invited his closest followers.
  Then he tells his disciples,
    "With desire I have desired to eat this
    Passover with you before I suffer."

It was no accident
  that Jesus chose the Passover as his setting.
  The Passover meal was, and still is,
    a family event.

Large families gather
    for feasting and celebration.
There is a ritual in which a young child asks,
    "Why is this night different
    from all other nights?"
    and the oldest man responds
        with the story of the first Passover,
            God's deliverance of the people of Israel
            from Egypt.

Jesus' last Passover supper was different.
    Jesus was not with his blood-relatives
            in Nazareth.
        He was with his faith-relatives
            in Jerusalem,
        a new family
            whom he had called to this table.
    He had two purposes:
        to celebrate with them the Passover
            that pointed backward to God's
            deliverance of Israel from bondage
            in Egypt and forward to God's
            promise of future deliverance;
        then to institute the Communion
            that would declare deliverance
            from spiritual bondage
                through the person and work
                of Jesus Christ.

This supper is a transition.
He whom we have seen so often as a guest
    now takes his place as host.
He deliberately shatters the traditional ritual.
    He passes the bread,
        perhaps with the usual blessings,
        but then he adds words never heard before.
            "This is my body, which is given for you."

What could he mean?
He takes the cup,
   and again he adds shocking words,
      "This cup that is poured out for you
      is the new covenant in my blood."
The disciples are puzzled, upset.
   What can he mean by "suffer,"
   "body,"
   "blood"?
They will not be able to understand
   until the Lord teaches them
      after the resurrection.

This is the transition
   from the last Passover supper
   to the first Lord's Supper.
The first Passover left behind
   the bondage in Egypt;
   ahead of it stretched the road to Canaan,
   the land of promise.
This last supper leaves behind
   the bondage of sin;
   it leads to the glory of God's new promises:
   redemption,
      salvation,
         eternal life.

The supper marks the transition
   from Jesus' bodily presence
   to the spiritual presence
      of the risen and ascended Lord.
From now on his presence will be made real,
   not in his physical body,
      but in a new communion:
      in the proclamation of the word,
      in the breaking of bread,
      in remembrance of one who said,
         "With desire have I desired
         to eat this supper with you."

The Ninth Meal

Emmaus: In Breaking Bread
Luke 24:13-35

Worship Focus

A large loaf of bread, broken in half and placed so that the broken surfaces partly show. There could be three plates at the table, with the broken bread in front of the center plate.

A Litany For The Ninth Meal

Leader: Great God of heaven and earth, we come to you in praise.

People: We celebrate the joyous news of Jesus Christ, risen from the dead.

Leader: Death could not conquer him.

People: The tomb could not hold him.

Leader: Yet we confess that at times our faith has been too small. Christ our Lord lives, but we have not listened for his word.

People: Our eyes have been upon ourselves, and we have failed to look for him.

Leader: We thank you that Christ came to the disciples in the garden, and on the road to Emmaus, and back in Jerusalem.

People: We thank you that in grace you have sought us and drawn near to us.

Leader: When we come to your holy table, Lord, we sense your living presence.

People: We have heard you in your word; we have felt your presence in the breaking of the bread.

All: May our hearts and minds be always open unto you. Amen.

Emmaus: In Breaking Bread
Luke 24:13-35

*Now on that same day two of them were going to
a village called Emmaus, about seven miles from
Jerusalem, and talking with each other about all
these things that had happened. While they were
talking and discussing, Jesus himself came near and
went with them, but their eyes were kept from recog-
nizing him. And he said to them, "What are you
discussing with each other while you walk along?"
They stood still, looking sad. Then one of them,
whose name was Cleopas, answered him, "Are you
the only stranger in Jerusalem who does not know
the things that have taken place there in these days?"
He asked them, "What things?" They replied, "The
things about Jesus of Nazareth, who was a prophet
mighty in deed and word before God and all the people, and how our chief priests and leaders handed
him over to be condemned to death and crucified
him. But we had hoped that he was the one to
redeem Israel. Yes, and besides all this, it is now the
third day since these things took place. Moreover,
some women of our group astounded us. They were
at the tomb early this morning, and when they did
not find his body there, they came back and told
us that they had indeed seen a vision of angels who
said that he was alive. Some of those who were with
us went to the tomb and found it just as the women
had said; but they did not see him." Then he said
to them, "Oh, how foolish you are, and how slow
of heart to believe all that the prophets have
declared! Was it not necessary that the Messiah
should suffer these things and then enter into his
glory?" Then beginning with Moses and all the
prophets, he interpreted to them the things about
himself in all the scriptures.*

As they came near the village to which they were going, he walked ahead as if he were going on. But they urged him strongly, saying, "Stay with us, because it is almost evening and the day is now nearly over." So he went in to stay with them. When he was at the table with them, he took bread, blessed and broke it, and gave it to them. Then their eyes were opened, and they recognized him; and he vanished from their sight. They said to each other, "Were not our hearts burning within us while he was talking to us on the road, while he was opening the scriptures to us?" That same hour they got up and returned to Jerusalem; and they found the eleven and their companions gathered together. They were saying, "The Lord has risen indeed, and he has appeared to Simon!" Then they told what had happened on the road, and how he had been made known to them in the breaking of the bread.

Who was this stranger who came up to us
    and interrupted us?
We had enough on our minds.
A week before, Jesus had come to Jerusalem.
    We went to hear him every time
        he came to the city,
        but he hadn't been there for months.
Usually he came quietly with his disciples,
    but this time was different.
    He came with shouts and a big procession,
        entered the temples and raised a storm
           with the thieving merchants,
        challenged the high priests
           and told parables against them.
Then came the terrible shock.
    Jesus was arrested;
        he was turned over to the Romans

to be crucified,
    with all the beatings and mockery
    and coarse brutality of the Roman
    soldiers and that terrible death.

Today the Sabbath was over,
    and it was time to go home,
        back to Emmaus.
    We walked the seven weary miles,
        tired,
            broken-hearted.
    We had enough on our minds:
        no Messiah,
        no hope,
        and this strange story
            of the women who said
            they found his tomb empty
            and had a vision of angels
                who said he was alive.

We were talking about Jesus,
    how we believed he was the Messiah,
    when this stranger came up to us
        and asked what it was all about.
    How could he intrude when we were grieving,
        talking of the terrible things
            that had happened?
    Where had he been
        that he had not heard of this?
    Yet he asked politely
        and seemed truly interested,
            so we told him all we knew.

We told him,
    but then he began to tell us,
        as if he knew far more of the story
            than we did.

He began from the words of Moses,
    teaching that the Messiah would come.
He said he spoke from the prophets,
    saying the Messiah would suffer —
        die —
        and would rise —
        enter into his glory.
    Prophet after prophet,
        he led us through the Scriptures.

Seven miles, seven sad miles,
    we walked with the strange teacher
        who seemed to know so much more:
            more than we had ever heard before,
            more than we had ever learned
                from the priests.
His words stirred us from within.
    Somehow his words lifted us up,
        and the miles did not seem as long.

Seven miles:
    we were home at Emmaus,
        late in the day.
We stopped at our house.
    He said, "Shalom," and he started on.
    "Stay," we asked him.
        "It's supper time and it will be dark soon;
            it's not time to travel on."
    We urged him, and he agreed.

Supper was simple;
    my wife had no time to cook.
We had a loaf of bread;
    there were cheese and dates in the chest.

Then it happened.
    I am the head of my house,

the host at the meal;
    it's up to me to say the blessing.
He looked at me,
    reached over,
    picked up the bread;
    and he said the blessing,
        as if it were his house.
He spoke as if he were speaking
        to his own father;
    and he broke the bread.

Then we knew!
    I'd seen those hands break bread before:
        break bread and pass it to 5,000 men.
    We saw his face.
    It was as if my eyes had been clouded
        all afternoon!
    Why hadn't I seen him?
    We saw Jesus.
        We knew it was he,
            no one else.
    It was Jesus — alive!
    He vanished,
        but we knew it was he.

Suddenly, it all fit together:
    his words on the way,
        explaining the Scripture;
    his hands at the table,
        breaking the bread.
    They were all part of one truth.
    He prepared us by opening the Scripture;
        he confirmed it by breaking the bread.

There was no staying at Emmaus.
    We rose up and walked back to Jerusalem,
        no longer tired,

for we had to tell the disciples our news,
joyous news.
We had seen Jesus,
risen and alive!
He came to us
in the teaching of the Scripture;
he was known to us
in the breaking of the bread.

The Tenth Meal

Broiled Fish
Luke 24:36-43

Worship Focus

A platter with a whole broiled fish fillet or a baked whole fish would be ideal. Someone in the congregation may have a mounted or wooden fish as a wall decoration, and that would be easier to take care of.

A piece of comb honey, though not in the newer translations, would pick up the line from Ezra Pound's poem.

A Litany For The Tenth Meal

Leader: Gracious God, Father, Son, and Holy Spirit, we praise you for the glorious resurrection of the Christ, our Savior.

**People: Christ is risen!
He is risen indeed!**

Leader: In his rising from the tomb, Christ has conquered the power of death.

**People: Christ is risen!
Christ is risen indeed!**

Leader: In his life and death and resurrection, Christ has opened to us the way of eternal life.

People: Praise and glory, honor and thanksgiving be to our God now and forever.

Leader: In his resurrection life, he has assured us of his living presence.

People: Praise and glory, honor and thanksgiving be to our God now and forever.

Leader: We thank you for the empty tomb and the meeting in the garden, assurances of his rising.

People: Worship and praise be to our God and to the living Christ.

Leader: We thank you for the signs of bread and fish, assurances of his reality.

People: Dominion and power be to our God and to the living Christ.

Leader: Christ is risen! Glory be to God for ever and ever!

All: Christ is risen! Alleluia!

Broiled Fish
Luke 24:36-43

Luke records ten meals
    that Jesus shared with people,
    and the tenth is a time of overflowing joy.

After the amazing, too-good-to-be-true
    report of the resurrection,
    Luke tells us of the two disciples
      who walked with Jesus
        on the road to Emmaus.
At supper, when he broke the bread,
    they suddenly recognized him.
They rushed back to Jerusalem
    to tell their glorious news to the apostles.
We pick up the story at that point.

*While they were talking about him, Jesus himself
stood among them and said to them, "Peace be with
you." They were startled and terrified, and thought
that they were seeing a ghost. He said to them, "Why
are you frightened, and why do doubts arise in your
hearts? Look at my hands and my feet; see that it
is I myself. Touch me and see, for a ghost does not
have flesh and bones as you see that I have." And
when he had said this, he showed them his hands
and his feet. While in their joy they were disbeliev-
ing and still wondering, he said to them, "Have you
anything here to eat?" They gave him a piece of
broiled fish, and he took it and ate in their presence.*

"A ghost!"
The disciples had just been exclaiming,
    "The Lord has risen indeed,
      and he has appeared to Simon!"

They had just heard that the living Jesus
    had been at supper in Emmaus.
But they had seen him killed;
    the resurrection was too far
        out of their human experience.
Of course they were startled.

They didn't need to speak.
    Jesus could see their fears,
        their questionings.
For weeks he had been telling them
    that he would be crucified
        and that on the third day
            he would rise again.
    They had already heard that he had been seen
        at least three times that day.
    What more would they need?
    What would convince them?

He offered his body,
    the print of the nails,
    a body somehow changed,
        but real,
    a body to be seen and handled,
        not a dream of their grief-stricken minds,
        not a vision of their fevered eyes,
        not a mass hallucination.
He offered the firm reality
    of the one who conquered death
        and rose again.

What more did they need?
    They believed,
        so there was joy;
            yet it was too wonderful to believe.
What would reassure them?

He asked for food,
    They gave him a piece of broiled fish,
        and he ate it in their presence.
Did his resurrection body need food?
    No!
    They needed the food.
    They needed to see him eat.
    A piece of broiled fish was something solid.
    They had eaten the other pieces
        of the same fish.
    They knew it was real.
    He ate to convince them
        that he was just as real.

Many of us know the King James version
    of the Bible with its added phrase,
        "and a piece of honeycomb."
That was not in the best old manuscripts,
    so it is not found in our newer translations;
    but Ezra Pound used it
        to make a true point in his poem,
        "The Ballad of the Goodly Fere."
        ("Fere" is an old English word
        meaning companion or mate.)

    Ha' we lost the goodliest fere o' all
    for the priests and the gallows tree?
    Aye, lover he was of brawny men,
    O' ships and the open sea.

    When they came wi' a host to take Our Man
    His smile was good to see,
    "First let these go!" quo' our Goodly Fere,
    "Or I'll see ye damned," says he.

Aye, he sent us out through the crossed
  high spears,
And the scorn of his laugh ran free,
"Why took ye not me when I walked about
Alone in the town?" says he.

Oh, we drank his "Hale" in the good red wine
When we last made company,
No capon priest was the Goodly Fere
But a man o' men was he.

I ha' seen him drive a hundred men
Wi' a bundle o' cords swung free,
When they took the high and holy house
For their pawn and treasury.

They'll no get him a' in a book I think
Though they write it cunningly:
No mouse of the scrolls was the Goodly Fere
But aye loved the open sea.

If they think they ha' snared our Goodly Fere
They are fools to the last degree.
"I'll go to the feast," quo our Goodly Fere,
"Though I go to the gallows tree."

"Ye ha' seen me heal the lame and the blind,
And wake the dead," says he,
"Ye shall see one thing to master all:
'Tis how a brave man dies on the tree."

A son of God was the Goodly Fere
That bade us his brothers be.
I ha' seen him cow a thousand men.
I ha' seen him upon the tree.

He cried no cry when they drave the nails
And the blood gushed hot and free,
The hounds of the crimson sky gave tongue
But never a cry cried he.

I ha' seen him cow a thousand men
On the hills o' Galilee,
They whined as he walked out calm between,
Wi' his eyes like the gray o' the sea.

Like the sea that brooks no voyaging
With the winds unleased and free,
Like the sea that he cowed at Gennesaret
Wi' twey words spoke' suddenly.

A master of men was the Goodly Fere,
A mate of the wind and sea,
If they think they ha' slain our Goodly Fere
They are fools eternally.
I ha' seen him eat o' the honey-comb
Sin' they nailed him to the tree.

Easter is a time for joy, overflowing joy.
　　There is mystery,
　　and there is reverent amazement,
　　but above all there is celebration,
　　　　for Jesus has risen from the dead!
Jesus did not leave his people
　　prey to doubts or uncertainty.
He used the supper to reveal himself,
　　to show them he had truly risen.
He took the broiled fish to reassure them
　　that wherever they were,
　　　　he would share their circumstances.
He came to their table
　　to lead them in celebration:
　　　　exuberant, joyous celebration
　　　　　　of the resurrection!

DATE DUE

due 4-10-00		
ILL# 7599845		
to. Alabam P. Lib.		
Service		
GAYLORD		PRINTED IN U.S.A.